I Wonder Why

Pyramids Were Built

and Other Questions About Ancient Egypt

Philip Steele

KING*f*ISHER

NEW YORK

KINGFISHER
Larousse Kingfisher Chambers Inc.
95 Madison Avenue
New York, New York 10016

First edition 1995
(HC) 10 9 8 7 6 5 4
HC - 4 (TR) / 11 98 / VAL / HBM (HBM) 150R400

Copyright © Larousse plc 1995

LIBRARY OF CONGRESS CATALOGING-IN-PUBLICATION-DATA
Steele, Philip, 1948-
    I wonder why pyramids were built?/ Philip Steele —
1st American edition
        p.   cm. — (I wonder why)
    Includes index.
    1. Egypt — Civilization — To 332 B.C. — Juvenile
literature   2. Egypt — social life and customs — To 332
B.C. — Juvenile literature.
[1. Egypt — Civilization — To 332 B.C.]
I. Title. II. Series: I wonder why (New York. N.Y.)
DT61. S866 1995
932–dc20 94-30244
CIP AC

ISBN 1-85697-550-9 (HC)
ISBN 0-7534-5050-X (PB)
Printed in Italy

Author: Philip Steele
Consultant: Department of Egyptian Antiquities,
    British Museum
Cover illustrations: Chris Forsey, cartoons by
    Tony Kenyon (B.L. Kearley)
Main illustrations: Peter Dennis (Linda Rogers Associates)
    14-15, 24-25, 28-29; Chris Forsey 12-13;
    Luigi Galante (Virgil Pomfret Agency) 4-5, 16-17;
    Nick Harris (Virgil Pomfret Agency) 18-19, 22-23;
    Adam Hook (Linden Artists) 8-9, 26-27, 30-31;
    Tony Kenyon (B.L. Kearley) all cartoons;
    Nicki Palin 6-7, 10-11, 20-21.

CONTENTS

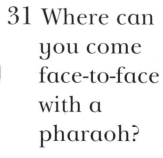

Why do we call Egyptians ancient?

We call the Egyptians ancient because they lived such a long time ago—not because they all reached a ripe old age! The first Egyptians were farmers around 8,000 years ago. Within a few thousand years, Egypt had become one of the most powerful countries in the world.

● Will people be studying us in 5,000 years' time? What will they think about the way we live now?

● The Egyptians usually built tombs for dead kings on the river's western bank, where the Sun sets. They believed that their kings went to meet the Sun god when they died.

● Egypt is mostly sandy desert, where nothing grows. The ancient Egyptians settled on the banks of the Nile River, where there was plenty of water for themselves and their crops.

• The ancient Egyptians didn't know about distant parts of the world. But they did explore parts of Asia and Africa. And their merchants bought wood, gold, ivory, spices, and even apes from nearby countries.

Why were the Egyptians great?

The Egyptians were so good at farming that they became very rich. They built fantastic temples for their gods, and huge pointed tombs called pyramids where they buried their kings. They had armies and ships and courts of law. Their priests studied the stars and their craftspeople made beautiful things from gold and silver.

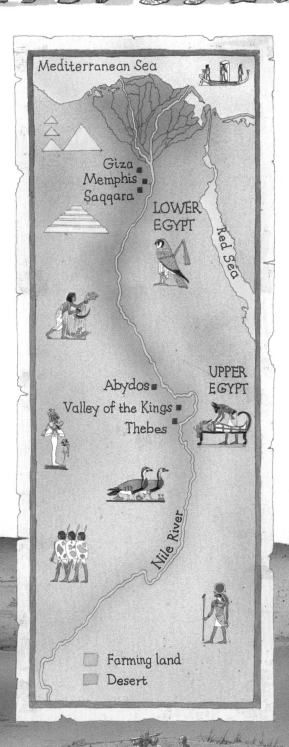

Mediterranean Sea

Giza
Memphis
Saqqara

LOWER EGYPT

Red Sea

UPPER EGYPT

Abydos
Valley of the Kings
Thebes

Nile River

Farming land
Desert

Who ruled Egypt?

The king of Egypt was called the pharaoh. The Egyptians believed that their Sun god Ra was the first king of Egypt, and that all the pharaohs after him were his relatives. This made the pharaoh very holy — and very powerful! The people thought he was a god on Earth.

● The pharaoh's advisors were called the Honored Ones. There were all sorts of royal officials, too, with fancy names like the Director of Royal Dress and the Keeper of the Royal Wigs.

Could a woman be pharaoh?

Although very few women ruled Egypt, there was a famous pharaoh called Hatshepsut. When her six-year-old nephew came to the throne, Hatshepsut was asked to rule Egypt for him — just until he was a little bit older. But Hatshepsut liked ruling so much that she wouldn't let her nephew take over. He didn't get the chance to rule until he was 30 years old!

● When she was pharaoh, Hatshepsut had to wear the badges of royalty. These included a false beard, made of real hair.

How would you know if you met a pharaoh?

He would be wearing a crown, of course! In fact, pharaohs sometimes wore two crowns at the same time—a white one for Upper Egypt, which was the name for the south of the country, and a red one for Lower Egypt, which was the north.

Who was the crocodile god?

In old paintings and carvings, most Egyptian gods and goddesses have animal heads. The water god, Sebek, was shown as a crocodile. Thoth had the head of a bird called an ibis, while Taweret looked like a hippo! Osiris and Isis were luckier. They were shown as a great king and queen.

● The Egyptians loved to wear lucky charms. Their favorites were scarabs. The scarab beetle was sacred to the Sun god Ra.

● The ancient Egyptians worshiped as many as 2,000 gods and goddesses!

Thoth, god of learning

Osiris, god of death

Who was the goddess Nut?

Nut was goddess of the heavens and she was usually shown covered in stars. Many gods and goddesses were linked in families. Nut was married to Geb. Isis and Osiris were their children.

● Being a priest was a part-time job. Most only spent 3 months per year at the temple, and lived at home the rest of the time.

BACK IN 9 MONTHS

● Priests had to wash twice during the day and twice at night, to make themselves clean and pure for the gods.

Taweret, goddess of childbirth and babies

Isis, wife of Osiris

Why did the Egyptians bury their mummies?

A mummy is a dead body which has been dried out so it lasts for thousands of years. The Egyptians believed that the dead traveled to another world, where they needed their bodies. And they didn't want any bits missing!

● Egyptian families had their nearest and dearest mummified, but it was an expensive business. Only the rich could afford a really good send-off.

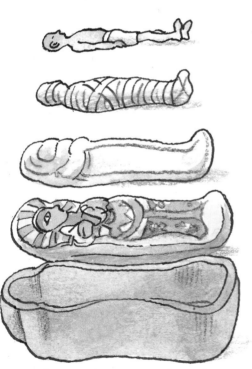

● The mummy was placed inside a series of wooden coffins. These were put in a big stone case called a sarcophagus.

● Monkeys, crocodiles, cats, and other sacred animals were often mummified, too!

Why were mummies brainless?

The ancient Egyptians believed that the heart was the most important part of the whole body. They thought that the brain was useless. So when they were preparing a mummy, they took out the brain.

Why were mummies wrapped in bandages?

Wrapping the dead body helped to keep its shape. After the insides were removed, the body was dried out for 40 days in a salty substance called natron. Then it was washed, rubbed with ointments, and bandaged.

11

Why were the pyramids built?

The pyramids were huge tombs for dead pharaohs and other very important people. No one knows exactly why the pyramids were shaped this way. Some people think they were built to point toward the Sun and stars, so that the dead person's spirit could fly to heaven like a rocket.

● The Great Pyramid at Giza was built more than 4,500 years ago. This is what it looks like today.

● Pharaohs were buried with all their finest clothes and jewelry, so tombs were given sneaky traps to catch out robbers.

● There are other, smaller pyramids at Giza, and more than 80 at other places in Egypt. Some have stepped sides and bent tops.

● This is what the
Great Pyramid
looks like
inside.

Pharaoh's
chamber

Who liked to get knee-deep in mud?

Egyptian farmers loved mud—it has all the water and goodness that plants need to grow well. The most important time in a farmer's year was when the Nile flooded and dumped rich, black mud on the dry fields. A good flood meant a good harvest. A bad one meant people went hungry.

● The only farm land in Egypt is near the Nile River. It used to be called the Black Land, because the mud left by the floods was black. The rocky desert was called the Red Land.

● Priests watched the Moon and stars in order to work out a calendar of the months. This told them when the floods would come and when to plant crops.

● Juicy grapes and fresh green vegetables were grown in the rich Nile mud. Golden ears of wheat and barley were harvested and stored in granaries.

Which was the fastest way to travel?

The quickest route in Egypt was the Nile River. Egyptian boats were made from river reeds or wood. They were the only way to get from one side of the river to the other—unless you swam and liked crocodiles!

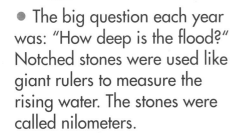

● The big question each year was: "How deep is the flood?" Notched stones were used like giant rulers to measure the rising water. The stones were called nilometers.

● Farmers dug ditches to carry water to their crops when the Nile wasn't in flood. They used a clever machine called a shaduf to lift water out of the river into the ditches.

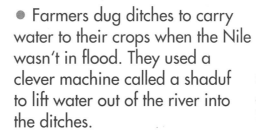

Why did people sit on the roof?

The roof was just about the best spot in an Egyptian house. It was cooler than indoors, especially under a shady canopy. People liked to sit and talk there, or play board games.

● Egyptian houses had flat roofs. Pointed roofs were invented in rainy lands, to let the water drain away.

● Most houses were made of mud bricks, but stone blocks were used for temples, tombs, and palaces.

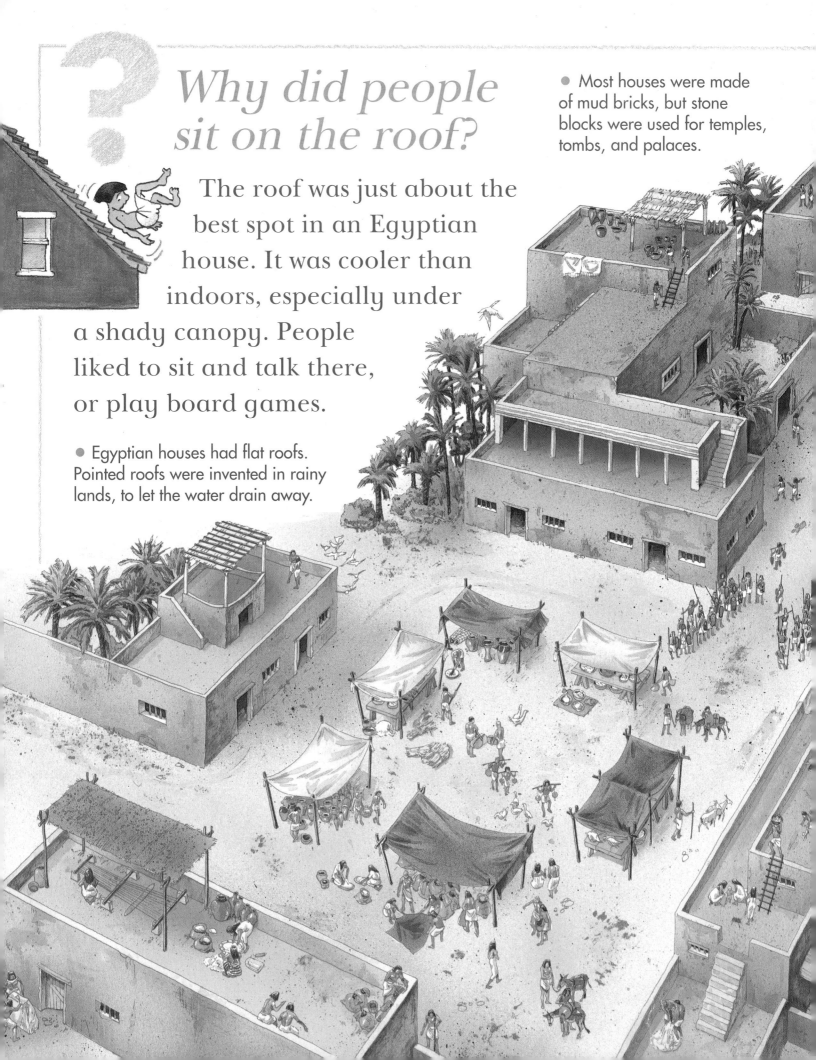

Who made mud pies?

Bricks were made
from river mud.
Brickmakers
trampled the mud with
their bare feet until it was sticky.
They added bits of straw and reed
to make the mixture firmer. Then
they shaped the mud pies into
bricks, which dried hard in the sun.

Who had nightmares?

Some Egyptians must have slept
well, but their beds do look very
uncomfortable! They were made of
wood, with ropes or leather straps
instead of springs.
And people
didn't lie on soft
pillows filled
with feathers.
All they had were
wooden headrests!

Who had floury feet?

When Egyptian cooks made bread, they sometimes jumped into a huge bowl on the floor and kneaded the dough with their feet. Let's hope they washed them first!

● Egyptian feet were good for making wine, too. Every last drop of juice was trampled from the grapes.

● The Egyptians baked lots of delicious cakes — doughnuts, pyramid-shaped buns, and cakes that looked like crocodiles!

What's the world's stalest bread?

Loaves of bread have been found in Egyptian tombs. No one has tasted them, though. The bread is thousands of years old and as hard as rock!

● Wooden lunch boxes full of meat and fruit were sometimes left in tombs, in case the mummy got hungry in the next world!

● Egyptian bread must have been a bit gritty, even when it was fresh, since many of the mummies' teeth are very worn down.

Who had splendid feasts?

Well, poor people certainly didn't! Pharaohs and rich people held fantastic feasts, where they ate juicy pieces of beef, mutton, or goose. The meat was sometimes barbecued, and served with crunchy onions or garlic, as well as spinach, leeks, peas, or beans. What was for dessert? Juicy figs, sweet melons, or pomegranates.

Who looked really cool?

Egypt is a very hot country, and in ancient times people kept cool by wearing as little as possible. Ordinary workers just wore a simple cloth around their waists. But for the rich, the coolest fashion was graceful clothes made from the finest linen.

● Linen is made from a plant called flax. It's very hard to prepare, but the Egyptians could spin and weave it into lengths of beautifully light and flimsy cloth.

● Acrobats and dancers just wore strings of beads!

● Women wore long dresses with shoulder straps. Men wore long kilts that hung in folds. Children often wore nothing at all.

Who liked to sparkle?

Most clothes were plain white, so rich people added color and sparkle by wearing beautiful jewelry made from gold and colorful precious stones.

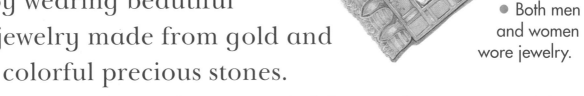

● Both men and women wore jewelry.

Sometimes, for a special feast, they wore wide cloth collars decorated with leaves, wildflowers, or glasslike beads. Poorer people's jewelry was made from copper and shells.

Why did shoes wear out?

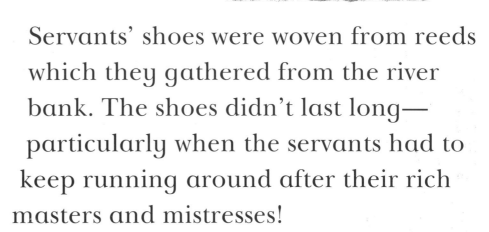

Servants' shoes were woven from reeds which they gathered from the river bank. The shoes didn't last long— particularly when the servants had to keep running around after their rich masters and mistresses!

Who loved makeup?

Rich Egyptian women wore lots of striking makeup. Eyeshadow went on first, then a black line around the eyes, and finally a rosy lipstick and cheek blusher. The ancient Egyptians still look beautiful more than 4,000 years later — in their paintings!

Why did women wear cones on their heads?

Rich women pinned cones to their wigs for feasts and parties. But they wore cones of perfumed grease, not ice cream cones! As the greasy cones melted in the warm evening air, they gave off a sweet perfume.

• The Egyptians loved to smell good. Rich people used scented oils and breath fresheners, and they carried sweet-smelling flowers around with them.

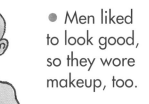

• Men liked to look good, so they wore makeup, too.

Who made a beeline for wigs?

Pharaohs and rich people—everybody who was anybody wore a wig on his or her head. The wigs were made of real hair, which was tied into hundreds of tiny braids and held in place by sticky beeswax.

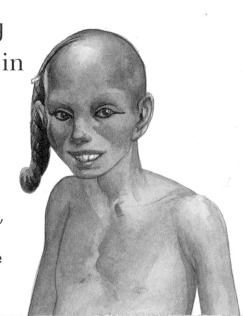

• The Egyptians took great care of their looks. They mixed up lotions to stop baldness and dandruff, as well as pimples!

• Young boys' heads were shaved, except for a single braid of hair on the right-hand side.

Who played with lions?

Nobody did, if they had any sense! But young children did play with wooden lions and other toy animals. Children also had spinning tops, as well as balls that rattled, and dolls with beads in their hair.

● Few people could read, so after a day's work they probably sat down to listen to storytellers. There were many exciting tales about gods and goddesses.

● Children ran around playing ballgames or tag, then cooled off with a dip in the river.

Who played board games?

● Experts think that the game of senet was a bit like Parcheesi.

Tutankhamun became pharaoh when he was only 12 years old. He loved playing a board game called senet, and after he died a board was buried with him in his tomb. It is a beautiful set made of white ivory and a black wood called ebony.

Did Egyptians like parties?

● Musicians plucked harps, beat drums and tambourines, blew pipes, and shook tinkling bells.

The Egyptians might have spent a lot of time building tombs, but they weren't miserable! They loved music and dancing. At rich people's banquets, there were often shows with dancers, musicians, acrobats, and singers.

Why is paper called paper?

Our word "paper" comes from papyrus, a tall reed that grows beside the Nile. The Egyptians discovered how to use the thready insides of these papyrus reeds to make a kind of paper. It was thicker than the paper we use today, but just as useful.

● Papyrus was expensive because it took so long to make. Quick notes were scribbled on pieces of pottery instead.

1 Papermakers cut and peeled the reeds.

3 They hammered them until the sticky plant juices glued them together.

4 Next they used a smooth stone or a special tool to rub the surface of the papyrus paper smooth.

2 They cut the reed stems into thin slices and then laid them in rows, one on top of the other.

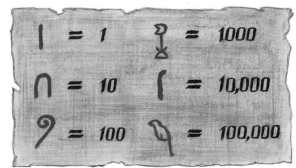

l = 1	**𝑞** = 1000
∩ = 10	**𝄐** = 10,000
𝟿 = 100	**𝕽** = 100,000

● There were even pictures for numbers. It can't have been easy doing math!

● Few children went to school. Some boys trained as scribes—people whose job was writing. They had to learn more than 700 hieroglyphs. Spelling tests were a nightmare!

What did Egyptian writing look like?

The first Egyptian writing was made up of rows of pictures, called hieroglyphs. Each picture stood for an object, an idea, or the sound of a word. Many of the hieroglyphs are quite complicated—they must have taken ages to draw!

● The ends of reeds were frayed to make paint-brushes. Ink was made from soot or red earth.

5 Finally, all the pieces of papyrus paper were glued into a long strip and rolled into a scroll.

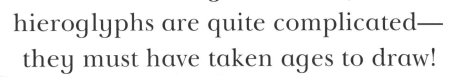

● These hieroglyphs make up the name CLEOPATRA. Perhaps you can work out how to write TOP CAT or POLAR.

C L E O P A T R A

Which were the most dangerous animals?

Egypt wasn't always a safe place. Wild bulls and lions lived in the desert, while hungry crocodiles lurked in the Nile River. Many Egyptians enjoyed hunting these animals, even though they could be dangerous.

● Even hippo-hunting could be dangerous. An angry hippo could easily overturn one of the hunters' tiny boats.

● When it died, a pet dog was buried with its collar—all ready for a walk in the afterlife!

Did people have pets?

Rich Egyptians had pets, just as we do today, and they loved them just as much. Most people settled for a dog or a cat, but people who really wanted to show off kept pet apes and monkeys.

● Today there are no lions or hippos left in Egypt. They are only found in countries far to the south. But ancient Egyptians would still recognize birds such as the ibis and the hoopoe.

● The whole family went along on duck hunts. The birds were brought down by sticks, which were a bit like boomerangs —only they didn't come back!

● Ostriches were hunted for their large tail feathers. These were made into beautiful fans to keep rich people cool.

What did Egyptians call their cats?

The Egyptian word for cat was miw—a cross between a mew and a meow! The Egyptians were probably the first to tame cats. They used them to catch mice in grain stores.

How can you become an Egyptologist?

Egyptologists are people who study ancient Egypt. To become one, you need to learn all about the history of Egypt, and the things that have survived from that time. Reading books and visiting museums are the best ways to start.

● Howard Carter went to Egypt in 1892 and spent many years excavating ancient Egyptian tombs. He made his most famous discovery in 1920—the tomb of the boy-pharaoh Tutankhamun.

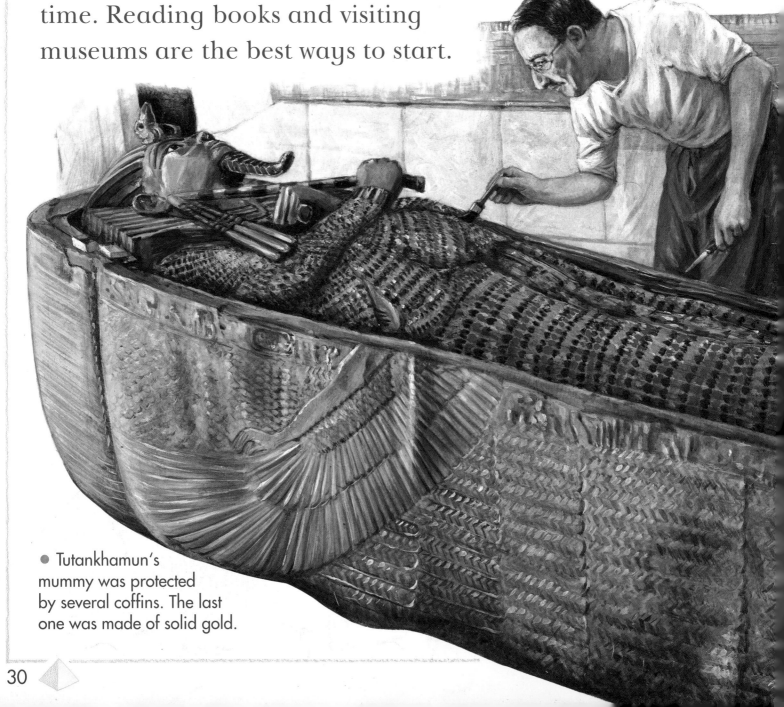

● Tutankhamun's mummy was protected by several coffins. The last one was made of solid gold.

Why do mummies have X rays?

Modern science is a great help to Egyptologists. X rays can show whether a mummy died from an illness or an accident. They can even tell whether it suffered from toothache!

● Egyptologists can even run tests on the things they find in a mummy's stomach, and work out what its last meal was before it died!

Where can you come face-to-face with a pharaoh?

Egypt's largest museum is in the capital city of Cairo. Here, you can gaze on the 4,000-year-old faces of the mummified pharaohs. Not all the pharaohs are here, though. Some are still lying peacefully, hidden in their desert tombs.

Index

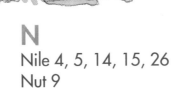

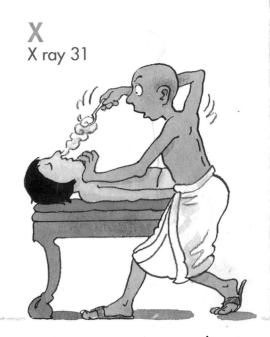